The Key

to

Unlock Your Future

- by Unlocking Your Life Purpose

Martin Christian Heuvel

BASKET PUBLISHERS

Contact: contact@bookbasketpublishers.com

WhatsApp: +917021692010

Website: www.bookbasketpublishers.com

ISBN: 978-93-94838-42-0

USD 10/-

This book is dedicated to both my parents

Who brought me into the world

To my dad, Thomas Abraham Heuvel

who somehow discerned that my future destiny was
going to be a clergyman and a leader to the wider
community, and then purposefully set me up at a young
age with his clergymen friends;

and

To my mom, Annie Catherine Heuvel (nee Louw),

who reared me as an entrepreneur, prayed for me daily
and taught me the way to live.

Contents

✻✻✻✻

Acknowledgement

This book is the first in a ten-part series, "Purpose-driven Living", coming from a life-long journey and mission which could not have been made possible without the involvement of very special people in my life, stretching over four decades.

Both my parents, in their respective ways, played a major role in my growth, calling, and understanding of my life journey, despite the challenges we faced as a family.

The opportunity to discover myself and develop my potential from a young age, are accredited to the church I grew up in, the Matroosfontein Baptist Church in Cape Town South Africa. The congregation, not having had a pastor at the time, meant that I, as youth leader, was exposed to the challenges of adult life very early in my life, as I had to deal with the challenges of both the youth and their parents.

I then learnt about how to discover one's life purpose, and its critical importance of living the purpose-driven life, with greater success, when I attended a seminar on "Master-life" discipleship by Avery T Willis Jnr. In 1980. This changed my life, and it is guaranteed to change yours.

After having discovered my personal divinely predetermined life purpose, I pursued it with a passion, despite the many naysayers along the way who did not understand the new journey I was on. I thank those critical minds. It tested me and made me stronger in my pursuit. It built my character.

During the most difficult years of this journey, my then pa/secretary, Ms Vernita Mortlock, stood with me like a rock. Mr Johnny Scheepers' commitment to pursuing the lessons he learnt from me in his own life, was a constant encouragement. He died, "having fulfilled his life purpose in his generation."

I thank the many influencers that inspired me to follow my passion, without them even knowing the path I was on. Amongst them are people like the late Rev Edmund Roebert, Anthony (Tony) Robbins, Dean Graziosi, Peter Sage, Aarzoo Shah, Arfeen Khan, Irfan Noorani, to mention but a few. You were my constant inspiration. Without you this *Purpose-driven Living* series would not have been possible. Aspects of your teachings and influence are reflected throughout these writings.

Above all, I acknowledge God, the Creator of the universe who guided me.

Martin C Heuvel MA

****

Foreword

Endorsement

By Mkangeli Matomela

"The book on 'How to Discover, and Live Your Life Purpose' by Honourable Martin Heuvel is a response to the cry for righteousness, justice, peace, and love for the prosperous socio-economic wellbeing of all the people of God on earth. The current generation of the citizens and communities facing hopelessness, corruption, substance abuse, immorality, diseases, poverty, unemployment and inequality, desperately needs the inspiration and practical steps on How to Discover and Live Your Life Purpose.

Both young and old, will learn a lot from this journey of life guided by a life purpose-driven lifestyle of God's ordained son of the coming Great Afrika Nation of the kingdom of God.

The list of the awaiting topics shall go a long way to help many to shape their own purpose driven journeys. Life purpose-driven journeys shall encourage each individual citizen, family, community, and nation to live life in probity and building a better socio-economic wellbeing for all the people of God in Azania, Mzansi, our beloved country South Africa, Afrika and all new covenant nations, in humble submission to Almighty God.

Well done faithful servant of the Highest God. We hope that you soldier on until you have translated your School of Missions curriculum to develop and train young generation leaders who are called to become the incorruptible ethical servant Public Representatives directly representing and accountable to the citizens, families, communities, people, new covenant nations, for sustainable socio-economic wellbeing of all the people of God in the universe."

(Mkangeli Matomela is a South African citizen, a married family man, community and new covenant nations visionary leader of the gospel of the kingdom of God. He has served the people of South Africa as a Liberation Struggle Freedom Fighter, Professional Teacher, Trade Unionist, Member of Parliament, Speaker and Member of the government's Executive Council.

His activities involved taking part in the country's Constitutional Court's decision declaring the Electoral Act of 1998 unconstitutional. He is currently spearheading a 'Citizens Parliament' initiative.)

****

Preface

Is it true that every person on the planet was meant to live a life of abundance in terms of their health, wealth (financial freedom), and happiness? For many years I could not believe it, judging from the way most people struggled through life's challenges. These pages will shine some light on the question and hope to reveal the answers to this question you too may be asking.

Never in the history has there been such a cry of desperation from all corners of the world, and an attempt by a variety of people to help citizens to find their life purposes. The desperation came from watching and living in a world going through one crisis after another. creating a life of uncertainty, and a sense of hopelessness, by the current generation, as well as their concern for their children's children, and theirs.

People, everywhere are seeking desperately for solutions to ensure their future safety, financial and job security. The pursuit of knowing and living one's life purpose in responding to those crises became the most prominent talking point, as those in the self-development industry have proven it to be the primary reason for them to survive and thrive in this world. The words, 'purpose', 'passion', 'follow your gut', and 'desire' have become almost household words.

People started buying every book in the market on the topic to learn more about finding one's life purpose. The scores of books, especially on-line is proof thereof. However, the search for answers seems to be elusive as the public seemingly did not get the answers to their particular challenges in finding that life goal for themselves.

This book is an attempt to satisfy the hunger of **ALL AGES** in terms of responding to those overwhelming calls for answers, but *particularly* so for those in **THE AGE GROUP 18-35 YEARS,** who currently are facing a world of economic uncertainty at a time they need to ensure they are making the correct life choices in terms of their future careers, and job security. Making the correct life choices became critical, and vital. and knowing their life purposes became pivotal in their daily choices.

Why highlight the *millennials*, (those between 18 – 35 years) so much? Simply, because they are at the most critical stage of their lives where they need to make important life-changing decisions in terms of their future, probably more than others. The generation of 40 plus have the tendency to think that it is too late and uncomfortable for them to move out of their comfort zones, and have already settled, more often than not for the second best. Those 18 and under, on the other hand, are set on enjoying life, thinking there is still ample time, which there is not.

The opportunities of the millennials lend itself for challenges and change, and it involve choices such as planning their future facing a world of high unemployment, choosing the correct life partners, career / job security and ensuring the decisions they make today will bring them the financial freedom in their later years to secure a better future in their ageing years. They need to consider their offspring growing up in a costly world of brand name items the children expect from their parents so as for them to fit with the 'Jones and their peers. At the same time, they need to start thinking of leaving an inheritance of wealth to their children's children (if they're smart enough) in the harsh world they are currently living in and declining year after year. They need to be considering that their children and theirs may never be able to earn enough to buy a decent house, with the high cost of living and increasing inflation. Will they too become backyard dwellers, or worse still, sleeping on the streets?

Many have already lost hope and are living a life of disillusionment. Sadly, many have already decided to accept the status quo and settle for what they are experiencing, not seeing any prospects of change on the horizon. In my country, South Africa, alone the unemployment figure in this age group is 60% and increasing annually as matriculants enter the job market. At this age they stand a better chance of surviving the global crises if they make the correct life decisions. They are young enough to make career changes if necessary, and daring enough in taking risks. Many are young parents who can use these concepts to 'train their children in the way they should go', to avoid the pitfalls we are in at present.

An added dilemma in knowing how to find one's much sought-after life purpose is the fact that different authors and speakers, all have their different versions of how to find it, and yet adding little help to those desperately seeking to know how to find theirs. Meanwhile these seekers are bombarded daily with the importance of knowing their life purposes if ever they were going to be successful in this world of economic uncertainty.

Some, who are living wealthily, and claiming it is because they follow their life purpose as being the secret, claiming it as being so simple, making everyone else who do not seem to have it altogether, feel stupid. There is a school of thought that believes that finding one's life purpose is simply by knowing what you are passionate about. Another school of thought being advocated is to follow your gut or your heart's desire. I disagree. Passion, gut, and desire are certainly important, but only after you have clearly established what your life purpose is, and that you are indeed heading towards your life destination, here on earth.

Those who were lucky enough to be successful in life because of them pursuing their life purposes often found theirs by luck, or accident. Some could have inherited it from their forefathers. To my understanding it is neither luck, nor accident, nor passion or desire. It is the providence of God their Creator, who divinely allowed it to serve a greater purpose in the universe. Whether or not they serve that purpose is a story for another day.

This book approaches the topic from a completely different angle, not mentioned at all by anyone else I have come across. My premise is that each one of us were conceived of by our Creator with a DIVINELY PREDETERMINED (note these two important words) life purpose, and were born with all the necessary gifts, talents, personality and abilities to carry out on earth that predetermined life purpose. This was to serve the needs of, or compliment the functions of the universe, and its inhabitants, which in turn you were already endowed with, such as everything necessary to make life possible for all living on the earth.

This book is a practical guide, based on the premise of your life purpose having been divinely predetermined by the One who created you. You were then conceived in your mother's womb for that purpose, and having been endowed, and born with all the abilities necessary to fulfil your life purpose on earth before you die. You are then guided to observe all the signposts that pointed towards your life purpose which you were oblivious to.

This book together with books two and three being foundational, and the remainder in the "Purpose-driven Living" series will also show you in practical terms how you can find your personal divinely predetermined life purpose, and goals, stay on course by making the perfect life choices, and end up living a more than abundant lifestyle, as well as being able to leave an inheritance of wealth to your children's children, and theirs, no matter what country you are living in.

To start with, the book will help you understand the difference between a life purpose and a life goal, a distinction not mentioned elsewhere

What is a Life Purpose and how do one distinguish it from a Life Goal?

"Life Purpose"

"A life purpose is an overarching objective to be accomplished in one's lifetime. It provides direction for everyday activities and determines our priorities".

It is the reason for my existence – *WHY* I am on the earth, what my Creator determined for me to BE when He formed me in my mother's womb. It is the role I have been elected and destined to fulfil in His plan on the earth. It is what people will remember me for and it is my total life testimony.

Vision of life purpose: Having a clear picture in my mind of my life ambition as it relates to my life purpose. It is the clear vision of my life purpose, which covers my relationship with my Creator, others and myself. It is my "bill board revelation" to use the phrase of Myles Munroe.

"Life Goal"

"Life goals are convictions about what my Creator would have me DO as I move in faith with Him to achieve His purposes on earth". It is therefore more specific than the life purpose itself.

Whereas the life purpose is intangible, the life goal is tangible. Whereas having reached my life purpose can only be determined that I reached it at the end of my life, my life goal/s are the tangible proof that I indeed have accomplished my life purpose at the end of my life journey on earth.

After you have established what your 'life purpose' is, you need to know HOW best to carry it out in your major life decisions, such as ministry, career, life partner, etc, through life goals. "My days are ordered by the Lord" says the psalmist. My Life goal helps me order my day-to-day priorities.

I will share my life journey and show how understanding one's divinely predetermined life purpose also simultaneously addresses the provision for carrying out one's life mission. The understanding and acceptance of the truth of both one's life purpose and that everyone was born with finance-generating gifts and talents, and when properly nurtured can even lead to a life of abundance and financial freedom can be anyone's reality.

It is in the understanding of the above, together with a clear step-by-step practical guide that makes this book different from many others.

It also links the dots in terms of one's personal divinely predetermined life purpose to the global challenges of the world and the answers to solving many of the problems facing the citizens of the world, including their impoverishment and poverty. It is the absence of knowing and living one's life purpose that causes the entire world to have persons in positions of power that they are unable to be successful in. They are 'square pegs in round holes', unable to solve the world's problems, and instead the cause of the global crises.

For easy reading, cost effectiveness and availability, the books are written in small chunks of ten in the Purpose-Driven Living series. However, the first three are a trilogy, and can be purchased as such, or in singles. At the end of every chapter there is a list of practical questions and suggestions, under the title, THOUGHTS TO PONDER. I trust it will be helpful as a workbook to make its contents relevant to the reader.

In no way is this book meant to provide answers to all the issues raised, but rather for it to serve as a discussion document which could help to provoke dialogue and constructive debate.

Martin C Heuvel MA

Educator and Life Purpose Ambassador

****

Introduction

Is this book on the topic of life purpose really different from the others, I am hearing someone is asking. This question I asked myself many times when contemplating writing it, which actually delayed writing this book for many years. What have I to offer differently to the many other more accomplished authors?

Then the second list of questions came to my mind. Why are almost all the motivational speakers, millionaires and even comedians these days driving the point home of finding one's life purpose as being so critical if everyone is going to be living a meaningful life of financial freedom, health and happiness? What do these successful global citizens have in common that they are so passionate about the topic and what is the connection, if any, between living their life purpose, and their wealthy lifestyles? If it changed their lifestyles so dramatically what can be the significance of it to the world?

What was I missing? I have been teaching the importance of knowing one's divinely predetermined life purpose from a biblical perspective to a primarily religious audience for more than thirty years with little success. In my search for the answers to my own questions, I embarked on several self-development courses. I started listening to the experts on wealth, health and happiness and soon discovered how easily blind-sided one can be if isolated from the real harsh world, and I started connecting the dots.

I soon realised that my narrow view of people finding, and living their privately, and individualised life purpose without it being seen and practised in the wider context of society, and the world is the cause of my short-sightedness and little impact on society. I discovered that there is a clear connection between living one's life purpose, and financial freedom, and that the two were intricately linked together.

I further realised that the many books on the market give very little, if any specific guidelines as to how exactly to find one's life purpose, hence the search for more on the subject of purpose, and because of the demand, more and more books were written, and published. The hunger was there but the nourishment lacked as the answers were clearly not meeting the "how to" needs.

As an educator, I started my research on how to connect the so-called dots. How can I make my knowledge, and experience relevant to the challenges the world is facing, if life's purpose is such an important factor in the world according to these prominent influential persons? How does life purpose contribute to their wealthy lifestyles, if any? Stay with me to find out.

I began with an analysis of those I trained, and discovered those who were the only one's really showing success, including financially, were those who practised living out their life purpose in the real world of sport, entertainment, business and politics. Having listened to the political activist pastor, Dr Martin Luther King Jr. sharing his famous speech, "I have a dream", struck a chord with me. I realised that unless knowing one's life purpose even as a Christian, and not serving others through helping out in changing people's circumstances, lacks the motivation for finding their personal life purpose.

We were created for others and were given the "power to create wealth" to impact society, and the wider world, through living out our divinely predetermined life purposes. Without this life goal of knowing one's life purpose makes little sense, hence no motivational speech can talk you into it. In fact, any selfish reason to do so lacks the motivation for it in the long run. Millionaires and billionaires will all tell you that to have sustained their wealthy lifestyles depended on what people, like the self-development gurus, Tony Robbins, Peter Sage, Arfeen Khan and others call the importance of 'contribution' and serving others.

I have also realised that the reason for the chaos the world is in, is because of people not knowing their own life purpose, and because they were not 'wired' for the jobs they were in, creating an even greater mess of the job. This I discovered became a culture over many years, appointing "square pegs in round holes" in every sphere of society, negatively and detrimentally impacting society globally, and having contributed to the misery of the millions of unemployed, and impoverished masses, and the state of the world as we see it today. The current crop of world leaders has proven that they do not possess the skills to solve the problems facing the world. Everything is in a mess, from the economic crises to saving the starving masses, from the environment to the global pandemics, from managing the global resources, to solving the corruption.

For many years there were cries that both the global, and national crises are the result of poor leadership by those who govern specifically but also generally everywhere else. In South Africa cadre deployment of those who were part of the struggle for liberation were to benefit in the new dispensation, regardless of whether or not they were fit for purpose. The leaders simply found it expedient to continue the global tendency of deploying *"square pegs in round holes"* regardless of the consequences and without any regard for the suffering masses.

Naturally, like everywhere in the world, there were other factors that contributed to the poor service delivery, ineffective leadership, mismanagement, and power-hungry people. Character flaws, hidden agendas, and corruption (because of the depraved state of man) became evident.

The one thing, however, that no one ever questioned, seemingly anywhere, is finding out whether a person is 'called' and accordingly skilled to hold particular positions of power in life. One's divinely predetermined life purpose designed by the Creator of the universe, who created all people with a specific life purpose was never a consideration, not in government or anywhere else, least not in religious circles. Similarly, those in power for obvious wrong reasons were not entrepreneurially so wired to share such skills with the impoverished masses.

About two decades ago this reality surfaced when professional life coaches were deployed by large corporate companies to find out the best persons for a job in terms of their giftedness and personalities. Unfortunately, it was done only with the top echelon of management and executives to ensure greater effectiveness in companies, and their bottom lines. Head hunting was introduced when new staff were needed. Sadly, this process did not filter down to middle and lower management, and the workers on the floor to which the same criteria should have applied.

Appointing *"square pegs in round holes"* went ahead unabated in spite of lessons one could have learnt from team sports. It would have caused teams like soccer or rugby to lose matches and when national pride was at stake, there would have been outcries especially from national boards to 'fire' coaches who dared to play their players out of their selected, and gifted positions. Imagine if a player like the world-renowned international soccer star Lionel Messi's giftedness was ignored and for whatever reason it was expected of him to play in a position he was not gifted for, and his team lost an international world cup final match as a result. Imagine the national outcry of his countrymen. In such events, *"square pegs in round holes"* would have been unimaginable, yet this lesson was not learnt and practised in other key positions of power. Many directors, executives and managers would have been fired had this been the case. In church circles this is still allowed, tolerated and practised, and so it is in all other government departments such as education, health, policing, housing, economy, etc. having *"square pegs in round holes"* appointees and we wonder why we live from one crisis to another. All over the world this is evident in all spheres of society as we continue to ignore the Creator's design for His created human beings, so purposefully designed for the greater purposes of the universe He created, for the sustainability of all man-kind.

From my own experience of more than 40 years doing public service as an educator and having travelled the world, I am of the opinion that only once the right people, gifted and called and trained accordingly to be fit for purpose are in positions of power, can we expect a different outcome in terms of responding to the myriads of problems the world is facing. Making the correct decisions favouring the masses will be the natural outcome.

Is this not what the world needs in these times of uncertainty and crises? Can we not imagine a different world in the future when those leading the citizens of the world globally, and locally are doing so from a position of their life purpose calling?

It is an injustice to the poor, the unemployed and starving masses for those in power to continue on this trend without a glimmer of hope of a better future for the citizens of the world, and their next generation. These masses are dependent on decisions by those people in power.

This writing is an attempt to prove that this can be done with a new belief system and mindset of the right leaders in power, together with the correct humanitarian support which involves restoring the dignity of all citizens. It is not a matter of race, religious persuasion or class. It is however incumbent on the 5% wealthy, who control the world's resources to play their part. The world as we know it, can become a better place for all its citizens in generations to come if we put the right people, called and equipped according to their divinely predetermined life purposes in their respective positions of leaderships of power.

It is a sad fact that unless we all change our mindsets from continuing the culture of forcing *"square pegs in round holes"* amongst others, and become aware of the possibilities, and are willing to change, all of us will go down the drain, including those who are wealthy and in control of the 95% resources of the world. This can prove to be a win-win situation for all and for the benefit of our children's children and theirs, both for the poor and the wealthy

In the book I hope to share how it can be done.

A Future Hope for The World is on The Horizon

Is change in our world possible? Can a new generation of purpose-driven leaders, called and fit for purpose help change the trajectory of the global scene currently on its way to disaster be stopped? I believe so if we act now and do it speedily and with commitment and passion.

While I was studying for my Master's degree in the human sciences, I had to write an assignment on 'Leadership in my culture'. Coming from the indigenous people group in South Africa I have been grappling with such issues for many years. In one of our group discussion sessions, discussing my paper, I asked my professor the following question:

"Prof, do you think I will see a change in my generation? The professor, twenty years my junior, responded. "I don't think so, in fact I will not see it even in my generation".

He paused and then continued,

"That does not mean you must stop doing what you are doing now, do it for the sake of your children's children. If you look for tangible evidence of change now, you'll be disheartened and stop what you're doing. Build now for the future, have in view a different world for your future generation, do your part today, for their sake".

I realised the value in what he said. I gave deep thought of my six grandchildren and the many grandchildren of other granddads and the future grandchildren of each of those reading this book and all those children now growing up. What will their future be like if the culture of "square pegs in round holes" continues unabated?

Will our grandchildren be able to afford proper dwellings to live in or will they too end up living in the backyards of others or on the streets or in squatter camps (ghettos) like many already are now doing? If the current scare of lack of food security is not addressed by the current wealthy leaders in power, will they have food to eat? What about the future of AI and the fear of a lack of job opportunities for them if in South Africa the unemployment rate amongst the youth is already 60%? Will the "rich get richer" and "the poor getting poorer" tendency not create an even greater dilemma, and will the thought of starving masses not overtake my grandchildren in twenty years' time?

Naturally, such a global or even a national change cannot be expected in this generation, but it does not mean planning for the next generation cannot commence. Nothing is achieved without first having had a thought, growing it into a vision and making a start no matter how distant it may seem and how impossible it looks.

Those holding positions currently as *"square pegs in round holes"* will obviously feel threatened, and will do everything possible to hold on to their ill-gained positions of power especially when they control or benefit from the world's fiscus for selfish gain. However, it is inevitable that at some point they will be unable to continue to live forever and a new generation of leaders will eventually replace them. We can determine what that new generation of leaders look like. Our future can look different when we start this mind shift change now, when we ourselves first undergo a new mindset based on a new belief system, and we prepare the next generation of visionary leaders. We do this starting with ourselves, in our homes with our children, grandchildren and youth, and wherever we have influence, and become the influencers of change. With this in mind there can be hope for our youth and the next generations.

'That is a pipe dream that will never happen', I hear the naysayers say. Maybe for some it will be "too good to be true". For them it will be as they believe, but for others it will instil within them a new hope to live another day, and even if the entire world will not change, my world and the world of my children's children will be changed, and so it will be for all who seek to follow suit. How? You ask. I will elaborate on it in this book, and in a series of books to follow.

I like the quote of world-renowned motivational speaker Les Brown, "If someone else could have achieved it, so can I" and he did, even though all the odds were against him from birth. Several others have proven it coming from disadvantaged backgrounds, people like comedian Steve Harvey, preacher and author, T. D. Jakes and many more. Many others currently living in abject poverty can too, if given a chance in life. If environments are more conducive for the victims to arise from the ashes, by those in positions of power and influence and if they understand their purpose in life, and being concerned for the dignity of their fellow citizens, nothing is impossible.

May I also remind you of the true saying, "Rome was not built in one day" and that no one gave South Africa a chance for a new political dispensation from the apartheid era without a civil war. And what about the breaking down of Germany's Berlin Wall that divided the west from the east? Who gave that a chance? And what about the collapse of the former communist Soviet Union? No friends, citizens of the world, there is hope for a better world under new leaders who live out their divinely predetermined life purposes and goals, leaders called "for a time such as this' ', leaders from whatever origin and background seeking the highest respect of others. These potential leaders are amongst us, others are 'out there', to be identified and developed according to their respective life purpose callings. When they understand the true meaning of predetermined life purpose and life goals, and are living out their full potential and giftedness which they were born with in all spheres of society, that situation is bound to change.

I have reminded ourselves earlier that it all starts with a single 'thought'. Whoever thought the Wright brothers dream (or thought) could eventually result in aircraft today flying all over the world. What about the thought of a computer, a mobile phone and the growing technological era, all started by one man's thought, or the light bulb that we use in our homes started with a thought? And so, you can think of others.

It was this conviction, if knowing, finding and living one's life purpose right where we are, correctly understood and in desperation and passion pursued can ensure a better life for all. Knowing one's life purpose, starting from childhood, properly guided by parents, career guidance during high schools, ensuring the correct choices of life partners and seeking employment or entrepreneurship that supports their life purpose journeys, is what this book is all about.

You, reader can be where it all start in your corner of the world, you finding your divinely predetermined life purpose and be the influencer in your concentric circle of concern, rallying around you like minded family and friends, start enjoying the benefits and influencing the appointments of people in important life positions affecting you.

Overview of the Journey

From the very offset it must be clear that it is a journey we are all on. In spite of the journey having an ultimate destination (life goal) what is more important to realise is that it is what we become on this journey that will ultimately take you there.

In reviewing the challenges, I came to the following conclusion and hope my suggestions would bring some clarity and provide helpful solutions from my personal knowledge and experiences. It is intended to address both the local and global communities since it is an issue of universal significance and more particularly grandparents, parents, educators, and more particularly the millennials for the reasons mentioned. To my mind it is of such value and importance that it is deserving of taking whatever necessary *"uncomfortable action"*, to quote Dean Graziosi.

I have created my book to be a practical guide with clear outcomes.

It is intended to challenge the status quo to the point of making the necessary change to our belief system and mindset and leading to the necessary action of:

(1) Each individual realising their own divinely predetermined life purpose and the happiness and success it brings to the individual,

(2) Where and when we have influence, we encourage only considering people for positions of power, and influence in particular whether in church, school boards, community policing or government or anywhere else, but also generally.

Such appointees must understand and be willing to live purpose-driven lives in its totality. It must become their passion. It will help society at large to understand the value of having the right people leading us in all spheres of life and in the process stop the culture of *"square pegs in round holes"*, causing all the havoc negatively affecting our lives and livelihood.

Obviously, we will not be able to change the world of poverty in our lifetime or ever, for that matter. However, it does not mean we cannot attempt to change the world for some, especially those in our own families, communities and concentric circles of concern with the finance-generating talents that come with knowing, and using the knowledge we have.

In my book you will find the tools and learn the exact formula and strategies to know your personal life purpose, and be able to execute it with definite clarity, and direction to your ultimate destiny here on earth. These lessons come from my personal experience of more than 40 years working with both church and unchurched community people, some with greater success than others, depending on people's willingness to put 'skin in the game', and the ability to shake off their negative environment, always ready to discourage them enroute to their life goal destinies.

In addition to the above you will find the answers to:

1. Why exactly you were created, and conceived in the first place, and born to your particular parents in your specific environment, and country with the particular skin pigmentation and ethnicity and particular talents, gifts, abilities, personality, and are alive today;

2. Why you possibly suffered the particular difficulties growing up and survived against all odds;

3. How you can find your particular niche and life purpose and living a happy, successful and fulfilled life of abundance and financial freedom;

4. The connection between living your life's purpose and enjoying a life of financial freedom as a result. The Creator already deposited all the necessary abilities in you as the provision for your life goals, if monetized.

5. As a single person finding the right life partner, compatible, and in support of your life purpose;

6. Avoiding making the wrong life choices and decisions and instead making the right decisions taking you step-by-step towards your ultimate destination (life goal/s) here on earth;

7. The particular role of a woman finding, and living her own life purpose in a marriage relationship, avoiding the pitfalls that lead to marital break-ups, and divorce, yet serves her husband as 'help meet' in his life purpose;

8. Practical tools to help your children and loved ones on how they too can discover their respective life purposes, giving you, as motivation, practical real-life examples of world-renowned successful personalities to learn from, and to support the principles advocated in this book.

After reading the book you'll be able to remain in contact with me through personal sessions of coaching, and mastermind group sessions to further assist you in your pursuit of living a purpose-driven life, should you so wish.

A final thought. I'd like you to keep in mind my reference to God as the creator of the universe throughout this book is my personal belief and preference. The principles as set out here are universal and can be applied to anyone of whichever religious persuasion you are from. You need not be intimidated by my terminologies. You can choose to refer to God as the Creator or whatever you wish. Some prefer to only refer to the 'universe', others to the 'light within' or 'inner voice' or 'higher power'. You are at liberty to do as you wish. I believe that God, as Creator of the universe, is in ultimate command of the universe, often referred to differently because of their religious background, upbringing, convictions, or preferences. I respect all peoples' preferences and all religions, and I am sure you do too. (For those of the Bible-believing Christian Faith, who might have certain expectations of me, I have scripture references in support of all I've written and can make it available on request).

Chapter 1

The Challenges We Face

a. My Personal Story

My entire life in one way or the other resembles the providence of the Creator of the universe as my life journey was determined by circumstances and events, I had little or no control over. I share my life story with some nostalgia. Life, growing up during the years of apartheid in our beautiful country is not something one wanted to remember. Our family was part of many others who were forcibly uprooted by the government from the upper-class suburbs of Wynberg in the southern suburbs of Cape Town, and literally forced us to relocate to new areas still in the process of being developed because of the segregation policies of the apartheid regime. As painful as it was to be separated from friends, family, and neighbours, because of the colour of our skin, we had no choice but to try and resettle in areas far away from where we had access to public transport, schools and the business areas. I had some nasty experiences. I was only six years old, and just started going to school, and had to relocate to another school in an area, later called Goodwood, with no transport to get there. I had to walk many kilometres with older scholars I did not know. One day leaving class later than usual, I missed the walking 'bus' of friends and lost my way home. I started to panic, and walked in circles crying as I could not explain where we stayed. It got late and getting dark, I was hungry, and started crying even more, as no one could help me. Meanwhile dad got home from work and frantically left home immediately, worried about what had happened to his child and eventually found me by a sheer miracle. I could see the relief on his face. This was to be my first real experience of the impact apartheid had on us as a family, and me in particular. I started to hate white people which I never did when living amongst them before.

In retrospect, I have learnt that it is not what has happened to me but what has happened for me in preparing me to become useful to help others in the transformation of their lives. Discovering my divinely predetermined life purpose was crafted out for me by the creator using some of the most adverse circumstances to do so. The ancient writings that *"all things worketh together for good that love God and are the called according to His purposes"* only became clear in later years as the latter part of that verse, viz *"according to His purpose"* started making sense to me and has set me on the course which I am on now.

Childhood

As mentioned above, I was born on the Cape Flats in South Africa into a so-called poverty-stricken coloured disenfranchised community during the hard apartheid years of white oppression of the 'non-whites'. One of the townships where some of the 'non-whites were dumped to find their own way of life was then the township called Bishop Lavis. The houses were literally built in the bush where there were no roads at the time. Walking down the sandy paths was something I will not forget. In winter the cold morning weather caused my feet to swell and in summer the heat of the sun would burn my feet that I had to make myself cardboard sandals with string to get home after school. My feet still bear the scars of those days.

I grew up in poverty and in adverse circumstances

Being the eldest of five siblings most of the chores fell on me. I had to cut wood in the bush and make a fire for my mother to cook on. Life was hard on my parents. My dad had to walk many kilometres to get to the nearest bus as there was no transport from the township. These struggles caused many frustrations between my father and mother. The effects of us having been moved to that new 'home' under duress began to take its toll on them. Money now was scarce. Added to their frustrations were the fact that they were completely incompatible and clearly had no guidance as to how to handle their frustrations. Dad was a 'city boy' used to socialising and mom a homemaker from a farm in a rural area, far from the city life. They could not get along and eventually divorced, leaving me to help my mom selling cookies and ginger beer on the soccer fields to survive.

This is where my entrepreneurial skills started and were developed and played a critical role in who I eventually will become in later life. Looking back, I can see how "all things can work together if …."

During my childhood I also learnt the importance of sharing the little we had with others less fortunate. I befriended a boy who later became my best buddy. Watching him during school breaks, my friend, Donald, never ate anything. I realised how the same fate affected his family. They could not send him to school with lunch. I told my mother about him. Mom filled my lunch-pack with extras for my friend who never came to school with bread.

Very early I learnt the importance of 'contribution', a critical value that would later go hand-in-hand with knowing and living a purpose-driven life.

The one good thing my dad did, was having clearly sensed what my future holds in life for me. He somehow knew that his son was destined to become a leader in society and particularly a priest in the church he served as a layman. During school holidays he would take me to his priest and let me stay with him with instruction to his priest, Father Harris, to take me on home visits with him, driving me around in his Austin Cambridge car.

Soon I became aware of my life purpose calling on life although I did not understand it as such at the time. It was the providential direction of my Creator.

Youth

At one time dad invited me to the house of another rector of the church where he was looking after the house of the minister who was away overseas. He made me sit at the desk of the minister with a pen in my hand and took a photo of me. At the bottom of the photo, he wrote *"Acting Minister"*.

Dad clearly understood that his son was called and destined to be a minister in the church and that it was my divinely predetermined life purpose, and that dad had to nurture me into that calling, in spite of dad not being in my life at home. Dad showed a different attitude towards me than he had towards the other siblings. This I will never forget and forever treasure. Dad has set me up for a *"time such as this"* from childhood.

As my dad suspected, I soon became a leader in the local church amongst the youth and an educator in the Sunday school. I was quickly formally appointed as the youth leader and superintendent of the Sunday school.

As a young leader I thrived at studying to become a better equipped leader, something I am doing up till today, empowering myself.

Already during my youth years, I soon realised that I was born to be an educator and that educating others has to do with me understanding life's purpose and that the provision for living out one's life goals must be through one's own entrepreneurial skills and that the income from it should be to bless others. I had to teach this to others. My source was not to be the church where I served but God, the Creator of the universe and the universe will cooperate in this regard. My role was to be resourceful and not wait on the resources of others.

Young adult

During my teaching of young people in bible class I discovered how easy it would be to make the right choices if one properly understood the context of a certain writing of knowing the perfect will of God for my life. In another book in this series, I will explain that. Just to mention at this point that knowing your divinely predetermined life purpose is not possible if you separate it from understanding your talents and special abilities. It is 'putting the cart before the horse'. Understanding what your talents and gifts are is critical to knowing and living in the perfect will of your Creator God.

Without this understanding, making the correct life choices, whether a career or choosing a life partner is hardly possible. This is how serious knowing your divinely predetermined life purpose is. Had I known this earlier in my life I would have avoided making some seriously wrong choices.

How serious is this culture of making wrong life choices by not knowing and understanding one's life purpose that I learnt and wish to help our youth prevent doing? In working with young people directly for many years in preparing them for their future I have witnessed the following:

This culture,

1. Does not recognize the individual's divinely predetermined life purpose, and immediately rules out

the involvement in his future life decisions of his Maker, the Creator of the universe;

2. It consequently is an indictment to his Creator;

3. It ends up in the individual innocently abusing his talents and purpose. Myles Munroe is quoted as saying, "When purpose is not known, abuse is inevitable"

4. It keeps the individual in poverty since he will not see how his talents and giftedness is the Creator's means of him living a life of abundance.

5. Preventing them from seeing the abundance they are gaining in the process is to serve others.

This culture has destroyed nations all over the world. These precious young people end up becoming the 'Square pegs in round holes" and not living the life they always dreamt of, growing up.

Later years

As I considered my past life and seeing how we as individuals have contributed out of ignorance towards the calamities we are in as individuals, as families, as the church, as a nation and the global community, I felt like the Creator looking down on us and feeling the same pity he had on the masses, living *"like sheep without a shepherd"*, dying in our sorrows and helplessness.

Since I have learnt the lessons of knowing my own life purpose and pursuing it with passion, I have felt the burden of doing something about it. Too many who did not understand it, have questioned every decision I made. I was seen to be a disruptor as I refused to continue with what has become a culture of making wrong choices for oneself and the implications it has had for others. In the following pages

I will enumerate some of the consequences and challenges we are facing of making decisions not in line with our life purposes.

Furthermore, the driving force behind my passion is my six grandchildren. I need to be able to at least secure for them in this world of uncertainty and economic crises some financial security for them to secure for themselves a life of financial freedom which my grandparents failed to do. We are told in the scriptures to *"leave an inheritance to your children's children"*. This is what the infamous Rockefellers and others did. They have secured through registered trusts and other clever methods generational wealth which will ensure the future generations continue living in financial freedom. Similarly, the story of The Duke of Westminster explains how after nineteen generations, those descendants are still benefiting from wealth that was created perpetually over more than 400 years.

This will be covered in a future writing of this series of **PURPOSE DRIVEN LIVING.**

I hope that every reader will seek to do the same.

b. When Purpose-Driven-Living is Adhered to

What are some of the benefits of living a life according to my divinely predetermined life purpose? I've found the following to be true in my life and others:

- I found making daily life choices easier than before, saving me many unnecessary pain, heartaches and regrets. Every decision takes me closer towards my life goal destiny as I am driven by my calling and not by circumstances.

- I found that my happiness depends on myself and not on the good opinions of other people (GOOP) that are often confusing and conflicting because they do not understand my life purpose.

- It protects my sanity and mental health as I am focused.

- I know who I am

- It connects me with like-minded people and gives me a sense of belonging to my specific tribe.

- It resulted in me living a healthy lifestyle and slowing down the ageing effects on my body. People often judge me between fifteen and twenty years younger than my chronological age.

c. The Individual's Dilemmas

That living my life purpose comes with certain challenges is undoubtedly true but surmountable and it brings deep satisfaction knowing that the universe is cooperating with me and my creator is smiling on me. The following challenges I successfully overcome on a daily basis.

- I am often misunderstood and my decisions criticised, especially by my loved ones and colleagues who do not understand my life purpose. Living in peace towards them can be a real challenge. Ultimately when they see my successes they accept my choices, however uncomfortable they may be.

- I often have to take uncomfortable actions which result in uneasy relations, but these also fade away in time.

These challenges build one's character.

d. The Johnny Scheepers (Worsman) Story

The late Johnny Scheepers was one of my disciples I was proud to have as an example of living his life's purpose.

Arriving back from serving a prison sentence he accepted the Lord as his Saviour in the congregation I pastored. He was a keen learner and would write down everything he learned from me. Wanting to understand his life purpose as he saw me do, he would lap up every detail.

Because of his criminal record Johnny could not find a job. Because of my understanding that we all were born with certain talents and abilities that can be monetized, Johnny quickly latched on to these teachings. He discovered his gift of 'wors braai' (barbeque on fire) when he helped me with a function I had. He did so well that he soon became known as Johnny 'Worsman'. He soon became so popular with his produce that others invited him to 'braai' for them at their functions. Then he started his own 'wors braai' business. He did so well financially that he trained others and set them up to have other stalls for him. His business rapidly expanded beyond his ability to manage it. He then gave some of those businesses away to his staff to do their own businesses. He continued growing his business.

Johnny then studied theology at the college I started, namely the "Cape School of Missions". Over a period of 9 years led 80 teams on short term mission outreaches throughout South Africa and beyond the borders into other parts of the continent of Africa.

Johnny, at that stage also realised his life purpose was not his 'wors braai' business but the provision for his life goals which was establishing new churches. He became the leader of those outreach teams and started a ministry called "Operation Dewdrop" under my leadership.

This was Johnny's life purpose until a rather unfortunate premature death ended his life on earth. He virtually 'died in his boots', a characteristic all purpose-driven people will end up in as is told in the bible of 'King David, having fulfilled his life purpose in his generation and then he died'

Johnny's success story did not end there. Before his death his 'wors braai' stalls resulted in him having started two butcheries, selling the best quality meat. His wife and children joined him in this family business. He owned several vehicles and had a fully paid house valued at a million South African rands.

Johnny learnt the art of giving and helping others. At his funeral stories were told of people's refrigerators which were regularly stocked up with meat Johnny blessed them with. Johnny never asked for money to pay for his mission trips. His business paid for it. 'Wors braai' was the provision for his vision which was the start of his ultimate success.

The former convict became an entrepreneur then a successful business man living his life to the full because he knew and understood his divinely predetermined life purpose.

e. The global crises – Square pegs in round holes culture

An unwelcome culture.

This is a culture of placing people in positions they were not created for and could not be fully blamed for their failure in executing tasks they were not gifted for. I was born into it and do not know any other and therefore, like everyone else I had no reason to question this practice until I became aware of the dangers of it and started questioning its validity and justification for its continued practice at a very young age. This brought me into conflict with the powers that be in every organisation I got involved in, from church to politics.

On my journeys into the country and overseas I've come across many frustrated individuals who were expected by their parents and others to follow careers the parents have chosen for them without any regard of their children's wishes and left them unhappy. On one such occasion when visiting a wealthy family of parents who were both medical doctors, a young lady already in her fourth year of studying medicine came to me seeking advice. She desperately wanted to know how to get out of studying medicine, fearing her parents would put her out of the house if she quit her studies at that late stage, having wasted her parent's money. She was not prepared to become a victim of being a *"square peg in a round hole"*.

The Jewish tradition

Ironically, Jews seem to be the only people that do not subscribe to that norm. In a radio conversation with a presenter a Rabbi explained the scripture commonly used by Christians, very differently. "Train up a child in the way he should go and when he is old, he will not depart from it" means in Jewish tradition that the training referred to is much more than spiritual or character. It is about training a child from birth in the direction of growing holistically, including his future careers as he grows into adulthood. No wonder they are such powerful businessmen and skilled in the life of economics and have survived against all odds wherever they found themselves.

Can we not learn from them and from team sports that it is folly to expect people to do things they were not called for and neither equipped for?

These and many others not mentioned are the challenges we face in the world we live in because we have not bothered to find out why we are on the earth, living in this beautiful earth. It is clear that animal life is more aligned to the universe than us human beings. All we need to do is do an honest evaluation of where we came from and the purpose we are on earth.

Simply stated, all of us must discover our divinely predetermined life purposes and pursue it with passion and discover the fulfilment of a life we were all destined to experience in the universe.

****

THOUGHTS TO PONDER

1. The author shared his personal life story. Which of your childhood dreams and / or experiences came to mind while reading it?

....
....
....
....
....
....
....
....
....
....
....

2. Have you ever considered that your childhood dreams (night or day dreaming of your future) could be a signpost directing you to your life purpose destiny? If so, Explain here:

....
....
....
....
....
....
....
....
....
....
....

3. Which of the benefits of a purpose-driven lifestyle, mentioned by the author, would you like to experience, and why?

....
....
....
....
....
....
....
....
....

4. Which part of the story of Johnny (Wors) gripped your heart, and why?

....
....
....
....
....
....
....

5. A-HA! MOMENTS (Other insights to ponder)

....
....
....
....
....
....
....
....
....

Chapter 2

Success Stories

a. Personal Achievements

I have always been very reluctant to blow my own trumpet and was often criticised for it as it has deprived people from learning from me about the importance of living the purpose-driven life I taught others. However, for the purpose of the book, however loath to do it, I shall share some of the successes which were directly as a result of knowing my divinely pre-determine life purpose.

You have observed that I regularly refer to my 'divinely predetermined' life purpose. I did so for a reason. I believe that before I was conceived in my mother's womb, as the scriptures say, my Maker already predetermined my existence and life purpose on earth and deposited within me everything I would need to fulfil that specific purpose He designed me for, just as He did with every other living being in the universe. Why would man be regarded differently to animals, I argued. Then I read how the psalmist described exactly that which I argued about and it became settled in my mind that I have only one reason for my existence on earth. God predetermined my life purpose when He created me. Therefore, to be happy and live a meaningful and fulfilled life, I can only do so if I know that specific life purpose. This has set me on the course of wanting to know what that life goal exactly is and that is what this book is all about.

As stated earlier in the preface of this book, life goals are the natural outflow and tangible expression of one's life purpose. So, it was no coincidence that the areas of my successes all related to and were in line with my life purpose. Those outcomes that were not aligned did not show the same successes. Once I realised that, it changed my perspective in life about what came my way as offers of employment in particular, but also everything else. No job, whatever the pay and benefits could entice me to accept it if it was not going to enhance living my life purpose. If it did, I would probably have ended up in politics or some other lucrative business opportunity, outside of my life purpose and another statistic of being 'a square peg in a round hole' frustrating everyone around me, like millions around the world, are now doing.

My personal life purpose (overarching objective) is empowering others for the purpose they were designed for. My life goal (tangible and measurable) is to educate people through projects, programs and building institutions of learning in order to develop their life skills and setting them up for their successes, and where necessary to provide them the necessary infrastructures.

The successes I therefore have achieved are all educational related. I personally pioneered the Cape School of Missions, a practical vocational training centre, Started training centre campuses in our local areas in conjunction with other distant colleges. One such college was the Vision International College in Australia which was recognized by the South African Qualification Authority and who recognized their accreditations. Through this institution I could see some of my students earn up to NQF level 8 (National Qualification Framework) diplomas.

One of my students returned to his home country, Zambia to start his own college for those unable to afford the exorbitant university fees.

To have been able to qualify doing the above I returned to one of our prominent universities to do my master's degree at age 62 and graduated at 65.

Another of my successful life purpose related projects was using my entrepreneurial skills to identify potential entrepreneurs and develop them into small business owners. Through my own initiatives I could acquire a property which is worth more than 5 million ZAR today.

These achievements would not have been possible apart from me knowing and pursuing with passion my divinely predetermined life purpose, in spite of the challenges I had to endure and conquer in the process.

b. Successful Celebrities

It is a fact that different people end up almost by default in finding their niche in life. This happens through the providence of the Creator of the universe and they become highly successful without the help of someone teaching them the principles I lay out in this book. However, these are exceptions to the rule.

One of the signposts I will elaborate on is the very first one. The child will manifest special interests, talents and abilities which could be identified early in life of the child as being indicators of his or her possible life purpose. When so noticed by the parent or through other circumstantial providence and accordingly nurtured, has proven this to be true.

Some of the names we will look at are golfer Tiger Woods, music legend Quincy Jones, professional soccer stars Lionel Messi, Ronaldo. Many Millionaires ended up that way.

THOUGHTS TO PONDER

1. The author told his own story. What stories of your own came to mind while reading his story? What significance do you attach to it?

....
....
....
....
....
....
....
....
....

2. What lessons have you learned from the story of the author?

....
....
....
....
....
....
....
....
....
....
....

3. Is there a story from anyone you know that had an impact on your life? Explain:

....
....
....

....
....
....
....
....
....

4. Which celebrity's story stands out in your memories, whether entertainment, sports, or whichever, and why?

....
....
....
....
....
....
....
....
....

5. A-HA! Moments (Other insight to ponder)

....
....
....
....
....
....
....
....
....
....
....

Chapter 3

The Step-by-Step Process

a. My Story

My discovery of my life purpose started when, as I mentioned earlier, when I was 19 years old and already made a choice of a life partner when I was teaching a bible class group of junior high young people the scripture of how to live a life of abundance and pleasing to one's Creator. It was a popular scripture preached, but mostly quoted out of context as the remainder of that chapter was dealing with one's special gifts and talents one is endowed with. Pleasing one's Creator therefore is both living a life of honour together with understanding one's special gifts and talents. The one without the other does not constitute understanding one's divinely predetermined life purpose.

This led me to further studying into looking further at the practical implications. One example that came to mind was the question of whether it is then possible to please my Creator of making the correct choice of a life partner without first knowing my gifts and talents and how that will determine my life calling and marrying the right life partner. I further realised having made that critical wrong choice would naturally lead to all other wrong choices thereafter. If therefore, I do not consider both mine and the life purpose of the proposed life partner, will we not be incompatible? Will we not sooner or later find out that our different interests and personalities will eventually tear us apart and we end up in divorce? It is common knowledge that incompatibility has been seen as the major cause of divorce and family break-ups? It further led me to research the different roles in a marriage of the respective life partners if life purpose is not properly understood. The crises in marriage relationships and family break-ups became even clearer and obvious.

This and other examples made me think seriously about my own life purpose decisions. Further studies of other examples and examining real life situations of family break-ups confirmed this. This will be fully explored in a subsequent book in this series.

b. Defining Life Purpose and Life Goal

The definitions of both life purpose and life goal/s as well as the relationship between the two were set out in the preface of the book. Read it again at this point. Here it is for your convenience:

What is a Life Purpose and how do one distinguish it from a Life Goal?

"Life Purpose"

"A life purpose is an overarching objective to be accomplished in one's lifetime. It provides direction for everyday activities and determines our priorities".

It is the reason for my existence – *WHY* I am on the earth, what my Creator determined for me to BE when He formed me in my mother's womb. It is the role I have been elected and destined to fulfil in His plan on the earth. It is what people will remember me for and it is my total life testimony.

Vision of life purpose: Having a clear picture in my mind of my life ambition as it relates to my life purpose. It is the clear vision of my life purpose, which covers my relationship with my Creator, others and myself.   It is my "bill board revelation" to use the phrase of Myles Munroe.

"Life Goal"

"Life goals are convictions about what my Creator would have me DO as I move in faith with Him to achieve His purposes on earth". It is therefore more specific than the life purpose itself.

Whereas the life purpose is intangible, the life goal is tangible. Whereas having reached my life purpose can only be determined that I reached it at the end of my life, my life goal/s are the tangible proof that I indeed have accomplished my life purpose at the end of my life journey on earth.

After you have established what your 'life purpose' is, you need to know HOW best to carry it out in your major life decisions, such as ministry, career, life partner, etc, through life goals. "My days are ordered by the Lord" says the psalmist. My Life goal helps me order my day-to-day priorities.

c. The Possibilities – Benefits

Following on from the above it is clear the most important benefit of knowing and living your life purpose as a way of life is that you are protecting yourself against making wrong life choices that often ends in regrets and irreversible negative consequences.

Other benefits have been mentioned in chapter one

d. The challenges

How certain are you that you know and pursue your life purpose and you are heading towards your life purpose destination? Is your life goal/s an expression of and reflecting your life purpose?

Imagine you are climbing the ladder of your life. When you reach the top of the ladder you breathe out your last breath. You died having reached your final destiny on earth, you were thinking.

There are different ladders against several high-rise buildings. You decide which one you are climbing. The climb is long and steep. You face many difficulties over the span of your life. You win some and you lose some but you nevertheless keep climbing the ladder of your life. Eventually you near the top of the ladder. The higher and the closer to the end of your life is in sight. The steeper the more difficult the climb gets. You are near the top. The end of your life is near. You are about to give a sigh of relief and climb the last step and you stretch yourself to look on top of the roof of the building you climbed against, believing you were doing well. You gave a deep sigh of relief. You eventually made it successfully, but then read the inscription on the top of the roof reading, in big bold letters, **'WRONG BUILDING',** you cannot do life over. YOU MISSED YOUR LIFE PURPOSE. You realised you too contributed to the chaotic state of the world your children, and grandchildren will be enduring without you being there for them. You die miserable, having missed your divinely predetermined life purpose on earth, and never enjoyed the life you could have lived. You missed a life of enjoying a life of abundance, wealth, health, and happiness, without leaving an inheritance for your next generation.

The results of not knowing, and not living one's life purpose with a passion therefore, has far reaching implications for both the individual and corporate society. In fact, the world at large is impacted by it negatively. It is alarming and people your children and mine included are looking for a glimmer of hope. Can we offer some a little hope, changing the world for the ones and twos we are in contact with? Doing it for our future generation, our own children and grandchildren. Doing it for our family, loved ones and friends.

Here is a glimpse of what it means for society and the world we live in and what those we leave behind will face once we've gone, all of which are outcomes caused by the past and current "SQUARE PEGS IN ROUND HOLES", the so-called leaders governing the world. How long will we allow the powerful square pegs to control the powerless?

a. The entire world is being ruled and led by "square pegs in round holes", more often than not, not knowing what they are doing. Some are deliberately manipulating the systems for selfish gain. It is clearly evident by the chaos the world is in considering the impoverished masses in spite of a few wealthy families who control the world's resources. Nothing will change until this situation changes. Finding and living our divinely predetermined life purposes and seeing the called persons in those positions of power is one clear way out of this chaos.

b. People not knowing who they are and accepting the immoral and indifferent lifestyles, even if it is not in line with their traditional and religious belief systems, throw up their hands in the air in surrender to what is happening around them.

c. People, desperate for any job, ending up frustrated and ineffective in wrong careers, many so disillusioned and have already committed or contemplating suicide. Others suffer from psychosomatic diseases and some already died premature deaths.

d. It is predicted that South Africa with its 60% youth unemployment is sitting on a time bomb

e. Unhappy people in the workplaces doing jobs they were never called or equipped to do are frustrating everyone else.

f. There is a new resurgence of the 'tolerance' philosophy that killed millions of people in the past. We must become more tolerant of others, we are told. In the name of tolerance, we see wars being fought against the intolerance of others. The gay and lesbian movements are pleading for tolerance and legalisation of it.

g.The same situation of 'square pegs in round holes' frustrating progress, prevails in churches, schools, governments, universities and everywhere else. This culture has permeated every sphere of society for generations and no one seems to understand why we cannot get out of the crises we are in.

h.There has never been so many people becoming all kinds of life and niche coaches as the demand for guidance is increasing.

Naturally this is alarming but who can deny this sad reality. Can we not help some finding hope in these hopeless circumstances by each one of us filling the vacuum we allowed by not being what we've been called to do in each of our own corners of the world?

****

THOUGHTS TO PONDER

1. Considering your own life purpose, how would you explain the difference between your life purpose and a life goal?

....
....
....
....
....
....
....
....
....

2. What benefits would you like to experience?

....
....
....
....
....
....
....
....
....

3. What challenges do you anticipate, should you pursue a purpose-driven life?

....
....
....
....
....
....

....
....
....

4. What A-HA moments (Interesting and relevant insights to your life) struck some chords to you, while reading this chapter?

....
....
....
....
....
....
....
....
....
....
....
....
....
....
....
....
....
....
....
....

Chapter 4

Following The Process

One thing that stands out for me in the Tony Robbins teachings is the importance of following the process. To be successful in anything, there are clear patterns and processes to follow. Taking short cuts has never led anyone to success.

The process in finding one's life purpose is a simple and straightforward one and easy to understand and followed once you accept the possibility that it can be done and have an open mind.

No person would like to climb the ladder of their life. At the end of life, you find that you 'climbed the ladder against the wrong building'. Your creator will not either.

However, one of the most tragic things in life is the inability of most to unlearn the past conditioning and many motivational speakers, and life transformation coaches are currently spending endless hours to help address this challenge of changing old **belief systems**.

In the next publication of this series, I address this challenge, on how to prevent limiting beliefs from hindering purpose-driven living, under the title **"YOU ARE BEING HELD BACK BY YOUR LIMITING BELIEFS"**.

Knowing your future destiny and ending up where you are supposed to be in terms of your life purpose, virtually depend on **burying the past** and digging up your new-found future. The challenge however is that unless you know your future you will keep going back to your past. Unfortunately, there do not seem to be many role models of purpose-driven people around in line with what I am sharing here. This makes it a little more difficult for some to visualise something you have no role model of.

Burying the past therefore is the first step on the journey to discover your life purpose and goal/s once you understand the need for discovering it and have determined to change your former belief system in this regard.

How can I determine my specific life purpose and life goal?

a. Firstly, accept that you are no accident (whether or not you were born out of wedlock) as your Creator is the giver of life and that when you were conceived in your mother's womb, He already determined your existence and through whom He will bring you into life.

b. Secondly, since your Creator is just and 'no respecter of persons', accept that He would not have discriminated against you as not to deposit within you everything you would need to sustain a healthy and wealthy living as others already have proven to be and have.

c. Thirdly, accept that your Creator formed you in your mother's womb for a specific purpose and already deposited in you the exact wherewithal in terms of gifts, talents, abilities and personality type which you would need to fulfil your divinely predetermined life purpose and tasks you would need to perform in His universe. You are short of nothing. You came out of your mother's womb complete.

d. Fourthly, accept that you can therefore know your divinely predetermined life purpose and goal/s regardless of who your parents are, what they believe and that no one and no circumstance can prevent you from pursuing your Creator's plan for your life EXCEPT YOU YOURSELF.

e. Fifthly, believe that you have finance-generating abilities through one or several of your gifts that you were born with to serve as 'provision for the vision' and that you need not depend on anyone or any organisation or church to fund your life goal/s.

f. Sixthly, believe that your Creator has already put people on your path to help you find your life purpose and help you to turn your talents into provision. Look around and ask Him to show you the way. He certainly will as He did to me.

g.Seventhly, believe that your Creator has already positioned you through what is commonly known as His providence, allowed circumstances that you were not responsible for, some positive and others seemingly negative at the time, or what you could not have chosen, to prepare the way for your success. These will become unveiled only once you take the first step on your journey to discover His life purpose for you. It is a way of walking in faith and demonstrating your trust in your Creator and in some cases even risk in order to test your commitment to the journey.

h. Finally, and ultimately, with a belief in your Creator God as your source, nothing is impossible.

With This Belief System There Can Be No Stopping Anyone.

a. Here are the practical steps that have helped me and many others.

From the day you were born there was evidence of signposts indicating the road to your life purpose and life goal/s.

Regrettably these were not understood by the parents as indications of your future destiny simply because they were not taught this and missed recognizing these signposts.

As mentioned earlier the Jewish traditions followed this and the success of the Jews wherever they lived proved it. On the other hand, the rest of us were caught up in this culture of forcing 'square pegs into round holes.'

Those signposts showed up throughout the youth years of the person but because parents were oblivious to it, has further gone unnoticed and ended up in the young adult life making the wrong decisions and life choices when they reached the age of deciding their future. Many of those decisions regrettably became irreversible and that individual was now on a course of virtual self-destruction in terms of his/her divinely predetermined life destiny due to the wrong life choices made in innocence. From that point onwards all life choices were based on wrong premises and today the consequences are seen and felt wherever we go. This indeed is the sad reality which eventually led to the culture of "square pegs in round holes" plaquing the entire world and the unfortunate consequences of ignoring the order of the Creator.

Here are the possible signposts

1. Childhood

As stated earlier, the Jewish tradition followed a writing that says, *"train up a child in the way he should go and when he is old, he will not depart from it"*. This was also quoted and used in the Christian religious writings but the only meaning that was attached to it was about the spiritual training, completely different to the Jewish understanding of the text. To the Jew it referred to holistically, including the child's future life in terms of career, business, life partner choices, etc. as everything was to be part of the child's religious life.

Therefore, to train up a child would inevitably include the parents having a sense and understanding of the child's talents and giftings. Is it any wonder how the child Jesus at the age of 12, though born into his dad's carpentry business was not expected to also become a carpenter but was identified as a teacher from his earliest years, having been empowered and trained by his parents into knowing the Septuagint so well to be able to teach it to grown men in the temple?

Here is the lesson for us.

Every child born into the world must be seen as unique and special and seen and treated with the greatest respect as a gift to the universe and that the parents to which that baby is born has the responsibility before God the Creator to care for that child as such and be trained in the way he should go IN terms of his divinely predetermined life purpose from the day he is born. The parents must thus observe every action and predisposition of the child and learn about the child in order to guide the child towards what his possible future destiny in life might be. You may be holding in your arms a future president of your country. He/she might be a future Elon Musk or Albert Einstein or Nelson Mandela or Lionel Messi. Etc. Here are some interesting stories:

Tiger Woods was growing up choosing instead of playing with toy motor cars chose to play with his dad's golf clubs and more than that had a childhood dream he told his parents at the age of four that, "when I am big, I am going to beat the likes of Gary Player, Jack Nicklaus, Ian Palmer and the others". His dad never made it big in the golfing world but took his four-year old son's interest and words seriously and coached him from childhood and he became the golfing legend, having beaten those golfing greats. In a newspaper article in the Cap Times of July 26, 2006 he was hailed by journalist James Lawton who wrote, "Why Tiger is the greatest of all time -above Ali, Pele or Nicklaus". Whether it can be disputed is another matter.

Lionel Messi, it is said, refused to go to bed at night without a soccer ball in his arms. It was his grandmother who took him seriously. In an article she was quoted as having told him "One day you'll be the greatest footballer player in the world". Little did she know that her grandson would become the greatest even to grace the sport. Regrettably she died and couldn't witness her grandson achieve it all, the article was quoted as saying when the whole world went wild when Lionel Messi held the world cup trophy up high at the FIFA world cup final in 2022 against France for his country, Argentina,

Pele (Edson Arantes do Nascimiento) The great soccer star from Brazil. It was his mother's support of his childhood ambition to become a professional pilot. However, as fate would have it, (or was it the providence of God stopping him from becoming a pilot), Pele changed his mind from becoming a pilot when he went to the hospital to view the autopsy of a pilot who was killed in an aeroplane. Upon seeing the corpse of the pilot, he decided that his boyhood dream would cease. It was his father who realised that his son had been blessed with the supernatural talent for the game. The rest is history. Interestingly enough his name was chosen by his mother after the inventor, Thomas Edison.

Quincy Jones, The Hollywood legend and the composer of "We are the world" and singing the song with the world's top artists, a great musician, composer, actor was a case in point how God can supernaturally through his providence find a rascal and elevate him to the highest positions in life.

At age 11, this black boy, a poor, hungry and a thug broke into a store for a pie to satisfy his hunger. When inside the store he saw in the corner a dusty piano. He ping-pong on it and said to the piano, "This is for me and I am for this". The rest is history.

All three of my children are following the careers they clearly wanted to follow, exactly in the case of my two daughters, and in the case of my son indirectly. Carmen, growing up, would always pray when she was little for the hungry, the people living under the bridges and the sick children. Her dream was to become a medical practitioner solving the problems of the sick. Today, against all the odds stacked against her, she is doing medical research for a private company after having done nursing in several hospitals. Veronica was into administrative and organisational work from very young. Today she is working as a legal secretary for a large company of attorneys. Wesley, when he was little, became notorious for breaking up his toys and everything he would put his hands on, and then trying to put it all back again. Today he is fixing computers and solving information technological problems.

When you were little, growing up, what were you interested in? Have your parents guided and nurtured you towards your possible future career? Or did they force you into a direction of their choice, to fulfil a childhood dream they could not achieve because they were not allowed to. You must now live out their dreams and you are now miserable in your job.

Some Children who are very creative and innovative might be destined to become inventors, don't stop them. Don't kill their inquisitiveness. Some only want to tell stories and make it up, or build castles in the sand on the beach. Observe their interests and encourage them. You may see them as a nuisance now, scratching on everything. They may be an artist, or painter or designer in the making, and one day they may become your major income source like Lionel Messi, Tiger Woods, Pele, Quincy Jones, Elon Musk, or whoever.

Some only want to sing over a make-believe microphone. It might be an artist in the making. Some Teaching a class of chairs and dolls – a future teacher perhaps or lecturer at a university. That inquisitive child always asking too many questions, especially when you are so busy, might be a lawyer, detective or journalist in the making.

As the years go by these kids may become more clearer as they grow older and become aware of their surroundings and career options. Some children would never dawn the steps of the university. So what? Don't expect them to. There are myriads of other options more suited to their future and already becoming clear as they grow older. Allow them to grow into their divinely predetermined life purposes. As adults, be open to change. What we were told growing up may not be what your child needs. You as a parent become the inquisitive one. You start allowing the questions that irritated you as a parent when your child was growing up.

Be prepared to invest in their future. If they show interest in a particular sport, or arts entertainment, or whatever, support them, take them to the training sessions and pay for it. See it as investing in their future. It is about paying forward.

When they start grade 8 make certain their subject choices in grade 10 fit their future career directions. Engage with the school authorities. Protect your child from being forced into directions that would mess up their future choices. If necessary, change the schools who cannot accommodate subjects your child needs and they cannot offer. Alternatively get teachers after school hours who are specialists in their subjects BUT DO NOT COMPROMISE their future.

b. Tools to Help in The Process

Helping the child

In future publications of this series, I will be covering aspects of more specific challenges that need more in-depth explanations, such as, amongst others, how parents can help their children from birth in terms of the AI challenges, using the technologies already available.

Helping millennials and older adults

c. The Questionnaire

To assist adults in finding their respective life purposes, I have prepared a list of questions that, if honestly answered and with the correct analysis, can help them know with about 80% accuracy what their life purposes are. Unfortunately, there is no software available at this stage that can give the outcomes of the responses to the questions. However, the answers may be sufficient in most cases for the person to come to a rather fair conclusion, as I will explain at the end of the questionnaire.

I will however provide one free consultation to those who buy the book and need further assistance.

Practical Guide to Help You Discover Your Divinely Predetermined Life Purpose and Life Goals

This exercise can be very useful in helping you to determine your life purpose and destiny. Start off by asking your Creator God to bring back to memory those things you need to write down. Write them down as it enters your mind without questioning its correctness or wanting to justify your reasons for omitting any thought that comes to mind.

Be as detailed and specific as possible. Be absolutely honest; forget about being modest about your responses; look for the obvious; stay within the question asked. If an attribute applies to another section, write it down again. Do NOT try to justify or interpret your response or consider a thought to be silly or unimportant.

Here is your assignment:

1. Write down the understanding you currently have about your purpose here on earth.

2. Make a list of FIVE things you are **CAPABLE** of doing and ENJOY doing e.g., inherent abilities, talents and gifts (include hobbies and special interests.

3. Write down the **ACHIEVEMENTS** you had in life since childhood (include setbacks you have successfully overcome) – those actions which YOU feel are accomplishments and which resulted in personal satisfaction for YOU.

4. What are your **NATURAL INCLINATIONS**, that which comes very naturally to you to do. E.g., for some people singing is more natural than composing a song or vice versa; some people are more inclined towards theorising than taking action, etc.?

5. What are you **PASSIONATE** about – the one thing that will set your spirit on fire, become an obsession and give you the drive to jump out of bed in the morning and do? What makes the adrenaline pump and makes you happy?

6. What are the area/s of your life in which you received comfort – emotional traumas and **SETBACKS YOU OVERCAME** since childhood?

7.   What do you think are your **SPIRITUAL GIFTS**?

8.   Write down the **TRAINING** you have had, e.g., designing, nursing, PC, etc.

9.   Write down **WHAT OTHERS THINK** you do well, (both ministry and otherwise) e.g., counselling? baking? witnessing? etc.

10. Write down FIVE things **YOU HATE MOST** in life.

11. What were the (possibly divine) **PROVIDENTIAL** occurrences in your life – that which happened to you or your family over which you did not have any control, good or bad?

12. Write down your **CHILDHOOD DREAMS,** fantasies, and ambitions.

13. Write down **WHAT FIVE THINGS WOULD KEEP YOU AWAKE AT NIGHT**? Prioritise the top 3.

14. Write down what 3 things are YOU **MOSTLY CONCERNED ABOUT WHEN THINKING ABOUT OTHERS?**

15. List the 3 things you desperately **WOULD WANT TO AVOID HAPPENING TO YOU IN YOUR LIFE.**

16. Write down your **CURRENT LIFE AMBITIONS** (what you hope to accomplish before you die, whether or not you think it is achievable).

Carefully And Prayerfully Go Over the Above a Second Time and Add to it, Deleting Nothing You Just Wrote.

d. The Analysis - Understanding the Outcomes

As promised above I will give you ONE free consultation to everyone who purchased a book. All you need to do is that you send me proof that you did indeed purchase the book and send me the answers to your completed questionnaire to my email address, marking it FREE CONSULTATION. My email address is heuvel.martinc@gmail.com

I will reply with further information.

The key to this exercise is to prove to you that what is both in your conscious and your subconscious mind, together with your dreams, and the rest of your answers are useful signposts pointing you in a very strong direction of what your life purpose and possible life goals could be. After your consultation with me, you will be convinced you are either already on the right trajectory or you'll feel comfortable with the direction you discover.

THOUGHTS TO PONDER

1. Do you accept the fact that following a specific successfully proven process or pattern helps one get to your outcomes better? Have you experienced such success? Explain.

....
....
....
....
....
....
....
....
....

2. Do you consider your current belief systems a benefit or not in finding your life purpose? If so, Why? Explain.

....
....
....
....
....
....
....
....
....

3. What lessons did you learn from Tiger Woods, and Lionel Messi, concerning your own childhood, and why?

....
....
....
....

....
....
....
....
....

4. What thoughts came to your mind while reading this chapter which you would like the author to consider in his future writing on the subject?

....
....
....
....
....
....
....
....
....

5. A-HA! Moments (Other insights you received to ponder)

....
....
....
....
....
....
....
....
....

Chapter 5

Living The Purpose-Driven Life

A truly purpose-driven life, experiencing all the benefits thereof is a daily lifestyle. It is a belief system that finds expression in one's daily choices. I chose this life decision I am making because I know where I am going and this decision is taking me closer to achieving my life goal/s. Anything that would hinder my progress toward my life destiny permanently I shall avoid. However, there may be times when a choice which is not absolutely congruent with my destiny invites my assistance. This will be temporary as it may involve being a scaffolding to assist someone else building his own building. There may be other situations or crises that demand my immediate attention. This deviation from my normal life pattern is temporary.

Your testimony must be, *"I am absolutely convinced that I am climbing the ladder of my life against the right building. No distraction or any curve ball that is thrown at me will get me off this ladder, however difficult, inviting, or attractive. I am not driven by circumstances or the good opinion of others. I am driven by my life's purpose."*

This is the attitude of someone who knows his divinely predetermined life purpose, and who has a clear life goal/is to be achieved before he departs from this world. It was a mission accomplished for Jesus at the age of 33 on the cross when He cried out, "it is finished". Your age to die is not in your hands. Paul, the apostle, said before his death, that he has fought the good fight, his life mission was accomplished. He could die without regrets.

This is the way my life must end. When the angel of death calls, no matter my age, I must be as ready as king David was, "having fulfilled his life purpose in his lifetime." On my tombstone, the inscription will read, "Here lies the remains of Martin Christian Heuvel. He died having fulfilled his life purpose in his lifetime." My legacy of having lived according to my divinely predetermined life purpose will live on to remind others of theirs.

What will be written on your tombstone? The following is intended to hopefully guide you on your life purpose journey.

Having accomplished the first vital part of discovering your purpose-driven life is only half the battle won. As previously said, it is not measurable and therefore mostly put on the backburner and not taken seriously and more often forgotten. It is vague because it is not tangible. It is challenging because it is a nice thought to have, but no one can challenge you on it if you are not in the process of pursuing it. This happens to be one of the reasons why those passionate about the topic buy all the books on the topic of 'purpose', almost to just make them feel good that they are interested in it. They often talk about it and its importance because it is out in the public eye and ear all the time and they want to believe they are part of that tribe. Because it is these days the 'talk of the town' in many circles, because of it being spoken about so much by important people, we want people to know we are also part of it. They would even quote people like Myles Munroe, Steve Harvey, T.D. Jakes, Oprah Winfrey and others. They grasp at every 'straw' yet never able to reach their life purpose destinations. One other thing about it, it does not build your character knowing about it only.

a. Deciding on Life Goals

The only way to give substance to the talk about 'purpose' is to attach to its meaning through having a life goal or outcome, giving expression to it, something tangible, measurable and excitable.

Many have various goals or outcomes they want to achieve but if it is not an expression of and in line with their own life purpose it, it loses its attractiveness very soon, as it is often then some other person or organisation's dream they want to accomplish with your help. I personally know many people like that. They have a desire to do things in organisations and churches, but they are never consistent and easily give up on it and jump from one project to the other to be seen to be busy. Even churches struggle to get their members involved in what is considered worthy projects and ministries decided upon by church boards but without considering those members' life purpose goals.

It is a fact that when you do something you have decided upon because it interests you, you do not need someone else to stand behind you and motivate you all the time to do things. You cannot wait to get out of your bed in the morning to work on what you yourself is passionate about. I am not suggesting you not get involved with those projects or ministries but do so where it fits into your life purpose. Let it be an extension and expression of your life purpose outcomes.

One of the most important outcomes of pursuing what you like and is in line with your life purpose is your personal growth. Outcomes, "excite, motivate, and inspire us to take action and push our limits. Outcomes shape your character because they are set with your mental state of mind," says Arfeen Khan. Since it stretches your limits, it forces you to continue with self-education programs and studies. My personal growth is ascribed to it. It was the late educationist, Dr. Clate Risley who at one of his conventions said, "if you stop learning you must stop teaching." This has been one of my mantras for decades.

b. Decision-Making

How do I decide on such life goal/s or outcomes? you are asking.

The only person you should allow to be part of that discussion if you are unable to do so yourself, is someone who understands the importance of your specific life purpose and is willing to help you find that particular niche. A good qualified coach may be able to assist you to a point. The bottom line is that a person must know your understanding of your life purpose and how a life goal fits in it, or rather flow out of it.

Back to our definition, "life goals are convictions about what God (your Creator) would have you DO as you move in faith with Him to achieve His purposes of why He created you in the first place." After you have established what your 'life purpose' is, you need to know HOW best to carry it out in your major life decisions, such as career, life partner, ministry, etc, through life goals. Life goals help order your day-to-day priorities and help you avoid making wrong decisions. For every major decision like marriage, vocation, etc, you need to ask:

"Will this choice help me to achieve my divinely predetermined purpose in my life?"

If you set life goals without FIRST settling your life purpose, you often substitute your goals for your life purpose.

As in the case of Johnny Scheepers, it will not only be congruent with your life purpose but you will also realise you have God-given talents you were born with which are able to be monetized as the provision for your vision or life goal/s.

One other important fact about it, as I will explain from my experience, as was the case with Johnny, your Creator does not put demands on you bigger than your faith and where you are at in your personal growth and development, at the moment. Your Creator through the universe will guide you step-by-step as you grow in your faith in your Creator's ability to travel with you in this rather exciting and adventurous journey to eventual health, wealth and happiness.

c. What Precautions are Necessary?

It is unfortunately true that many people I tried to help and who got to fully understand the principles of knowing their divinely predetermined life purposes never achieved their life purpose objectives. This was primarily because they became unstuck on some aspect of pursuing their life goals/ministries. Of course, it was challenging as it required of them to accept, amongst others, that they are responsible for their own future in terms of their health, wealth and happiness and that their acceptance of submission, personal accountability for their own life goals, self-development, and self-sufficiency would be better than being spoon-fed. The major reason was their old belief system of how things were done in the past and their difficulty of unlearning the 'old'. Sad to say, many of them ended in outcomes that were disastrous. The lessons learned can be avoided through the following:

a) Acknowledge that "no man is an island" and that you can never go it alone. It is said, "go alone and you go fast but go with others and you go far."

b) Your environment plays a critical role in your life choices. If it is toxic, you become toxic.

c) Who you hang out with tells who you really are. Your associations with people will either make or break you. If your closest five people you associate with most are more negative than positive, you are the sixth one.

d) Accept personal responsibility for your actions. It is your life and your future that is at stake. You alone are responsible for your future. No one other than yourself can be blamed for your future.

e) Submit to a mentor, someone who has travelled the road you are on before and has a track record to prove you can learn from him/her.

f) Remain humble.

g) Practice gratitude daily.

h) Never stop learning.

i) Do not forget where you come from and how you got to where you are.

j) Contribution. Pay forward and help others along the way of your journey to wealth, health and happiness.

d. My Story

The above has been my story of how I discovered my life purpose and life goal/s and the lessons I learned on my journey thus far. It was also the story of the late Johnny Scheepers, and others, not mentioned here.

I am an educator and my life purpose was "Equipping others in the knowledge they would need in whatever profession or ministry they were destined for.", particularly from the point of their divinely predetermined life purpose.

How did I get there? I had no role models of purpose-driven people in my life growing up and no one taught me these principles. I can only ascribe it all to my Creator who have providentially guided my path and who allowed the universe to teach me through events and circumstances I had no control over. I am just amazed how things worked out.

I was severely criticised by friends, family, colleagues, and followers for my seemingly 'strange' modus operandi. I had an inherent sense that I was doing the right thing and was not deterred from parting with the way I was doing things, despite the criticism. Much later in my life I recognized there was a pattern in my life which helped me understand the 'method in the madness.' I also discovered I had more success than others in similar positions of leadership. For this too, I was both envied by some, and even rejected by others. People saw me as a disrupter of the 'old paths' which brought them to where they were at the time. Old belief systems dominated their thinking patterns. I soon realised that it was not worth fighting them. I could not teach those "old dogs new tricks." I was on my own, crafting out my own future with very little support from others. Those who did initially supported me fell by the wayside for the reasons I mentioned earlier under the topic of 'Necessary Precautions'. I stuck to what I discovered was bringing me success. I did workshops on 'Vision of Life Purpose and Goals' and later developed a manual for the students I was teaching. Some of the concepts and principles in the student manual are reflected in this book. I developed and wrote other supporting papers and handbooks on the subject, some of which will be published later in this series.

How has it all begun? Most of it started with my dad's intuitive inclinations that his son is destined for leadership in the ministry. I had no clue why, at such a young age he would pick me up from home on a weekend and during school holidays and take me to drive around with cleric, Father Harris and later when I got older placed me in another cleric's chair, taking a photo of me and writing underneath it 'Acting Minister.'

Thereafter, the strange and unexpected appointment of the then youth leader, the late Stephanus (Fanie) Engelbrecht, to suddenly resign and appointed me as the new youth leader at the age of 17, when the youth group consisted of people much older than me. I just finished grade 10 the year before, and had to seek employment to keep my siblings in school. The church had no pastor at the time and I had to assume the role of youth pastor and dealing with the adults as well when their children came to me for counselling about parental issues. I was thrown into the deep end and had to learn fast. Self-education became my priority and became a lifetime obsession, not knowing I was destined to become an educator.

An older youth leader in that denomination, John Cyster, took me under his wings. He and his friends were heavily involved in political consciousness during those early years of the apartheid liberation struggle. I was exposed to more than what I could handle at age 17. I had to grow up fast, still not knowing where it all was going to end up. Life was not easy as I just started working and became the bread-winner in the family.

This I later realised, was what I earlier repeatedly mentioned, the **providence** of Creator God. He had His plan for me in His universe well cut out. All that was left for me was to find it and pursue it with passion. All I did was follow the same tried and tested process of answering the questions I've written above. I soon discovered that the universe was ready and waiting for me to show up. This was to be my divinely predetermined life purpose,

'Equipping others for the role they had to play in terms of their specific career/ministry in the universe.'

Once I understood this, I only had to establish life goals congruent with my life purpose and tangibly expressing what it is the Creator desires me to accomplish before I depart from the earth. It is not that difficult. It was going to be done, within my limits, and in my particular context and where in the world He placed me. I became a man with a mission. This mission I still pursue with a passion after 40 years. I don't get tired. It gives me reason to get out of bed every morning. If you struggle getting out of bed in the mornings, you are not following your life goals.

How my life goals find expression.

My life goal, in short, has also become my profession. As an educator I am about educating people all over the world, especially in terms of them finding and pursuing their life purpose and goals and my goal/s are training or guiding them in all matters relating to their life goals, hence all I do, was and still is, and will be education related. How it is expressed is determined by the context and stage in life. My current expression is authoring books, coaching, counselling, and doing consultations in any way possible from where I live and are in life. Nothing except the method changes. I will be doing so till my dying day DV.

My ultimate life goal is to

Spend my retirement years educating citizens globally, (like Paul the Apostle did) from my retirement home, through my authoring of books and writing pieces of literature, and other ways of communicating the truth of the critical importance of knowing one's divinely predetermined life purpose and goals, amongst others, and that my income for the rest of my life would be derived from my entrepreneurial talents and gifts as the Creator has predetermined before my conception and birth.

This goal is well on its way to be accomplished. In fact, should I die today, it will be so in part.

Here are some of the expressions over the past many years that build up to this moment for me. It shows how the Creator is not in any way rushing us towards our ultimate life goal/s but nurturing us towards it in stages we can manage at any given time. I hope it will inspire you to start your own journey.

With hindsight it is now clear that already from my childhood, and throughout my life there were signposts I was oblivious to, pointing towards my ultimate understanding of my life purpose and life goals.

- Having been the firstborn and therefore the older one amongst my four other siblings has had its own significance in the journey, despite the fact that I was conceived as an unwanted baby.

- During my childhood schooling years, I already revealed a life of concern and compassion for my other poor and hungry friends, even though we were all in the same situation. 'Contribution' was at the heart of friendships from my childhood days.

- During my youth years, (I already shared the role my dad played, the early appointment as a youth leader, and my relationships with other older youth elders), I was invited to be the speaker at several different youth camps. My appointment of superintendent of the Sunday School at age 19 and the training of children's workers, was also significant. I travelled to all parts of the country and abroad to attend leadership training seminars and workshops as a consequence.

- I entered the theological college and graduated after four years with the Bachelor's degree, and as mentioned before, graduated much later with a Master's degree from the University of Pretoria. Studying was my passion to be better able to teach others.

- I pioneered a congregation in the township called Uitsig. Later I rented the nearby cinema building. Through my negotiating skills I later purchased the property from the local authorities. This was primarily for education purposes. The building was mainly paid for from funds raised through my entrepreneurial skills, my personal contributions and donations. Today the property which is valued at more than ZAR5m serves as part of my pensionable income through rentals.

- I was invited by the YOUTH FOR CHRIST director in Cape Town, David Kadalie, to assist the YFC with following up of young people and to join their high school "Impact" and "Insight" clubs in Uitsig.

- I was invited to become part of the local Interdenominational Youth Action movement and later served the local interdenominational ministers fraternal for 30 years.

- My passion for educating our people led me to start a Full-time Missions Training College (Cape School of Missions) which trained the former disenfranchised leaders from all over the country as well as students from the continent of Africa, at our premises. To secure full accreditation for our students I linked up with an accredited college in Australia, Vision International

College under Dr, Denis Plant. I trained other students from other colleges in our local campus such as Prof. Moodley (FBC) now affiliated to a university in Zambia, viz Gideon Robert University. I also lectured at a college on the local university campus founded by Dr. Winston and Dr. Charmaine Pienaar. I lectured on entrepreneurship to post graduates at the Good Hope Campus of False Bay College, in a nearby black township in Khayelitsha. It is too numerous to mention the achievements many of these students had on the global scene.

All of the above had direct relations to the topic. None of the impact I was able to make on the global scene would have been possible if I did not understand and pursue with passion my life purpose and these life goals.

THOUGHTS TO PONDER

1. Do you know people who are living their purpose-driven life? Who are they, and how can they assist you in living your purpose-driven life to the full?

....
....
....
....
....
....
....
....
....

2. Have you thought about what you would like to see written on your tombstone one day? What would you like people to remember you for? Write it down here.

....
....
....
....
....
....
....
....
....

3. Do you have any thoughts about which life goals in line with your life purpose you need to pursue? Write it here.

....
....
....
....

....
....
....
....
....

4. Having considered the life story of the author, do you think you might need the author's guidance and personal assistance on your journey?

....
....
....
....
....
....
....
....
....

5. A-HA! Moments (any other insights that you are pondering on)

....
....
....
....
....
....
....

Conclusion

I have often wondered what the world would have been like if people from all over the world in every generation knew and exercised their divinely predetermined life purpose, callings and goals. What a different world would we not have had? We would not have feared, as we now do, the kind of life our children's children would be facing when they grow up.

But since that is 'water under the bridge' let us look forward to a new world we can and hopefully we are going to leave for our future generations.

To make the book affordable and accessible to the masses I have not gone into the full detail of every aspect of what this topic deserves. Instead, I will be producing shorter, and more concise publications directed to specific areas of needs and to the persons who might be interested in only certain aspects of the topic. These will become available in the order of priority as the need for it becomes clear. The topic of life purpose and its full implications is a dynamic one and will only take its full effect over time. For this reason, I will be available to consult with whoever might be interested to interact with me about it. The hope is that sufficient readers will want to help in seeing this matter become a global movement of like-minded purpose-driven people. The following publications will be available as soon as the need is expressed for it:

Raising Superkids - for parents and grandparents on how best to help their children discover their life purpose.

Choosing right - for young people in the Gen x and Millennial age groups, currently in the phase of having to make the correct choices of careers and life partners and career guidance educators.

Transforming lives - through renewing Belief systems and mindsets specifically in relation to life purpose.

The Provision for the vision – Monetizing my finance-generating gifts and wealth creation to live out my life goals.

Accountable living – the role of mentoring, association and environment.

Hindrance to cope with – Detox the soul. Inner Healing through the healing of toxic memories.

Small group facilitation - lesson presentation – (an easy to follow nine-week lesson plan, using the scriptures to teach a small group on the subject of 'Vision of Life Purpose and Goals'.)

These are all specifically related to the topic in question.

 This book is intended to expose the real problem we are facing, it being the 'square pegs in round holes', people in powerful positions who, either have no idea what they are doing, or deliberately doing what they are doing to keep the powerless in the state of being powerless.

This culture is clearly manipulated and controlled by the 1% controlling the resources of the world, some directly, others indirectly, or even ignorantly.

Unless the rest of the world, including you and me, wake-up to how we all are making it possible and easy for them to perpetuate this culture by not insisting to further contribute to the status quo of being 'square pegs in round holes,' we are all doomed to suffer perpetually the current fate.

The place to start is to find your divinely predetermined life purpose and start living your life on your own terms in the universe. The Creator of the universe will always be in your corner when you do so, as you will be honouring His divine purposes for the universe.

I repeat, your contribution may not change the whole world but it will certainly change the world for your children and theirs, and who knows the future generations of others as well.

Let each of us reading this book, determine to find our divinely predetermined life purposes. Let us set our goals in alignment, and you and I enjoy life to the fullest, regardless of what's happening in the rest of the world, for now, at least, and hope and pray that the movement of purpose-driven-living people begins.

Martin C Heuvel

Email: heuvel.martinc@gmail.com

****

Appendix

Practical Guide to Help You Discover Your Divinely Predetermined Life Purpose and Life Goals

This exercise can be very useful in helping you to determine your life purpose and destiny.   Start off by asking your Creator God to bring back to memory those things you need to write down. Write them down as it enters your mind without questioning its correctness or wanting to justify your reasons for omitting any thought that comes to mind.

Be as detailed and specific as possible. Be absolutely honest; forget about being modest about your responses; look for the obvious; stay within the question asked. If an attribute applies to another section, write it down again. Do NOT try to justify or interpret your response or consider a thought to be silly or unimportant.

Here is your assignment:

1. Write down the understanding you currently have about your purpose here on earth.

2. Make a list of FIVE things you are **CAPABLE** of doing and ENJOY doing e.g., inherent abilities, talents and gifts (include hobbies and special interests.

3. Write down the **ACHIEVEMENTS** you had in life since childhood (include setbacks you have successfully overcome) – those actions which YOU feel are accomplishments and which resulted in personal satisfaction for YOU.

4. What are your **NATURAL INCLINATIONS**, that which comes very naturally to you to do. E.g., for some

people singing is more natural than composing a song or vice versa; some people are more inclined towards theorising than taking action, etc.?

5. What are you **PASSIONATE** about – the one thing that will set your spirit on fire, become an obsession and give you the drive to jump out of bed in the morning and do? What makes the adrenaline pump and makes you happy?

6. What are the area/s of your life in which you received comfort – emotional traumas and **SETBACKS YOU OVERCAME** since childhood?

7. What do you think are your **SPIRITUAL GIFTS**?

8. Write down the **TRAINING** you have had, e.g., designing, nursing, PC, etc.

9. Write down **WHAT OTHERS THINK** you do well, (both ministry and otherwise) e.g., counselling? baking? witnessing? etc.

10. Write down FIVE things **YOU HATE MOST** in life.

11. What were the (possibly divine) **PROVIDENTIAL** occurrences in your life – that which happened to you or your family over which you did not have any control, good or bad?

12. Write down your **CHILDHOOD DREAMS,** fantasies, and ambitions.

13. Write down **WHAT FIVE THINGS WOULD KEEP YOU AWAKE AT NIGHT**? Prioritise the top 3.

14. Write down what 3 things are YOU **MOSTLY CONCERNED ABOUT WHEN THINKING ABOUT OTHERS?**

15. List the 3 things you desperately **WOULD WANT TO AVOID HAPPENING TO YOU IN YOUR LIFE.**

16. Write down your **CURRENT LIFE AMBITIONS** (what you hope to accomplish before you die, whether or not you think it is achievable).

Carefully And Prayerfully Go Over the Above a Second Time and Add to it, Deleting Nothing You Just Wrote.

e. The analysis - understanding the outcomes

As promised above I will give you ONE free consultation to everyone who purchased a book. All you need to do is that you send me proof that you did indeed purchase the book and send me the answers to your completed questionnaire to my email address, marking it FREE CONSULTATION. My email address is heuvel.martinc@gmail.com

I will reply with further information.

The key to this exercise is to prove to you that what is both in your conscious and your subconscious mind, together with your dreams, and the rest of your answers are useful signposts pointing you in a very strong direction of what your life purpose and possible life goals could be. After your consultation with me, you will be convinced you are either already on the right trajectory or you'll feel comfortable with the direction you discover.

****

Bibliography

- Adelaja, Sunday, "Money won't make you Rich", UK Golden Pen Limited, 2016)

- Clason, George S., "The Richest Man in Babylon", (UK A Signet Book/Penguin, 1926)

- Coetzee, Coert, "Rich Mind Rich Man", (African Sun Media, 2009)

- Coetzee, Coert. "Let there be light on Wealth Creation" (African Sun Media, 2009)

- Daniels, Peter J, "How to be Happy though Rich", (Aus The House of Tabor, 1984)

- Dreyer, Hannes, Dr, "Power Goals –The Blueprint to go from ordinary to extraordinary" (SA Hannes Dreyer and Elzet Blaauw2020)

- Eker, T. Harv, "Millionaire Mind Online", (E-book T. Harv Eker, 2021)

- Eker, T, Harv, "Millionaire Mind Intensive", E-book T. Harv Eker, 2021

- Graziosi, Dean, "The underdog Advantage", (BBG Publishing, 2019)

- Graziosi, Dean, "Millionaire Success Habits", (PA Growth Publishing, 2017)

- Hill, Napoleon, "Think and Grow Rich", (UK Vermilion, 2004)

- Khan, Arfeen, "The Secrets to Becoming a Millionaire", (Arfeen Khan Performance)

- Khan, Arfeen, "The Secret Millionaire Blueprint", (Arfeen Khan Performance, 2007)

- Kiyosaki, Robert T., *Rich Dad Poor Dad*", (Scottsdale AR Plata Publishing, 1997)

- Kiyosaki, Robert T., "Second Chance", (Scottsdale AR Plata Publishing, 2015)

- Naicker, Jonathan Vincent, "Living Out of God's Pocket' (Quigney Jonathan Naicker Ministries,1998)

- Proctor, Bob "You were Born Rich", (Scottsdale AR Life Success Productions, 1984)

- Ricotti, Sonia, "Manifesting Money Blueprint" (E-book Sonia Ricotti, 2019)

- Robbins, Anthony, "Awaken the Giant Within", (E-book Anthony Robbins)

- Scheinfeld, Robert, "Busting loose from The Money Game", John Wiley and sons,2006)

- Wilson, Ann, "The Core Elements of Wealth" (E-book Ann Wilson, 2022

- Wilson, Ann, "30 Day Money Makeover" (E-book The Wealth Chef International)